RELAXATIONS

Published by
MAGINATION PRESS ®
American Psychological Association
750 First Street NE
Washington, DC 20002

Magination Press is a registered trademark of the American Psychological Association.

For more information about our books, including a complete catalog, please write to us,
call 1-800-374-2721, or visit our website at www.apa.org/pubs/magination.

Book design by Susan K. White
Printed by Worzalla, Stevens Point, WI

Library of Congress Cataloging-in-Publication Data
Names: Duch, Mamen, author. | Nieto Guridi, Raul, 1970– illustrator.
Title: Relaxations : big tools for little warriors / by Mamen Duch ; illustrated by Guridi.
Description: Washington, DC : Magination Press, [2018]
Identifiers: LCCN 2017052091| ISBN 9781433829048 (hardcover) |
   ISBN 1433829045 (hardcover)
Subjects: LCSH: Meditation for children—Juvenile literature. | Hatha yoga for children—
   Juvenile literature.
Classification: LCC BF723.M37 D83 2017 | DDC 155.4/1912—dc23 LC record
   available at https://lccn.loc.gov/2017052091

Manufactured in the United States of America
10 9 8 7 6 5 4 3 2 1

RELAXATIONS

BIG TOOLS FOR LITTLE WARRIORS

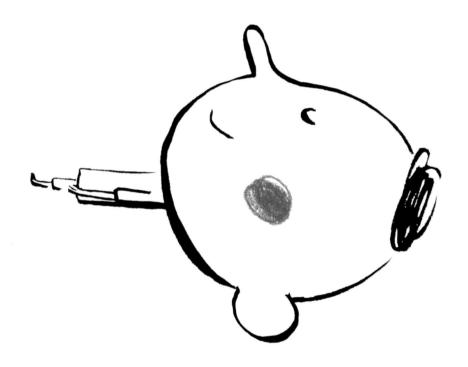

by MAMEN DUCH
illustrated by GURIDI

MAGINATION PRESS • WASHINGTON, DC
American Psychological Association

CONTENTS

How can we help our little warriors calm down and concentrate?

You may have heard the term *mindfulness*, or full attention. Techniques such as focused breathing, relaxation, and creative visualization are used to achieve a state of calm and concentration.

Creative visualization is the art of using mental images and affirmations to produce positive changes in our lives. It helps to bring to light everything that we have inside, everything that we can enhance and improve: confidence, self-esteem, concentration, intuition, creativity, and more.

Why not start using these techniques as children?

HELLO, LITTLE WARRIOR!

Would you like to play? Imagine that your mind is a huge movie screen. It is blank, and you can project whatever film you'd like onto it. Perhaps you can draw images that frighten you, or pleasant images that give you courage and help to bring out the best in you.

The good thing about this film is that you can go see it whenever you want and plus, it's completely free! You only have to give your imagination free rein and find a place where you feel good, such as at the movie theater.

Find a quiet place, and choose a comfortable position you can maintain for some time without moving: sitting cross-legged with your back straight, or perhaps lying on your back facing up. However you want. Close your eyes, and take three deep breaths.

Be alert, calm, and prepared to visualize your film. Do you want to be a piece of spaghetti? Or a butterfly? Or perhaps a shooting star that travels through space?

Silence, please. The film will now begin.

SPAGHETTI

1

Do you know what spaghetti is?
I'm sure you do. Try to visualize a piece
of uncooked spaghetti. Can you see it?
Well, now imagine that you are that piece
of spaghetti. Your body is stiff…

2

Now imagine yourself going into a pot, or
into a warm swimming pool full of bubbles…
mmmmm…

3

You'll begin feeling your body loosen up, loosening little by little, just like spaghetti after some time bobbing up and down in boiling water.

Feel how all parts of your body get looser bit by bit: your feet, your knees, your legs, your back, your waist, your chest, your hands, your arms, your neck, your head…they're all like boiled spaghetti.

4

Now you feel that your body is completely relaxed…

Al dente!

Ready to eat!

A SPECIAL TREE

1

You're sitting in a wide, green meadow,
looking at a tree right in the middle of it.

2

It's a very special tree: it has enormous roots
that go deep into the earth and a huge,
strong trunk that rises up to the sky.
Growing out of the trunk are many
leafless branches.
A sign hanging from a branch reads:
"I'm the Worry Tree. You can hang yours up
on me."

3

Think about something that has happened to you that you didn't like, for example: an annoyance, a disappointment, a fight, or a nightmare. Now imagine taking it off, as if it were a backpack or a jacket, and hanging it up on one of the tree's branches. Don't you feel so much lighter? It's as if you weigh less, and you're much calmer.

4

Look, up on a tree branch, a green leaf has sprouted! On it is written: "Make a wish."

Go ahead! Make one!

Breathe calmly. Be confident that, when the moment is right, your wish will come true.

THE BUTTERFLY

1

You're lying in a hammock, relaxed, swinging yourself slowly. You see a butterfly fluttering above you.

Focus on the color of its wings and how they move as it flies.

2

Suddenly, the butterfly lands on the tip of your nose. Keep still, and don't move a muscle! You wouldn't want it to fly away, would you?

Focus on how it opens and closes its wings slowly. *Open, close, open, close…*

3

You'll feel how your breathing slows down
and begins to follow the rhythm of the butterfly's
wings, getting slower and slower.

Open, close…

Inhale, exhale…

4

…until the butterfly closes its wings,
and it remains still, as if it were sleeping.

Do the same thing: rest, and imagine that you're
flying as freely and delicately as a butterfly.

THE FOUR ELEMENTS

1

Imagine that you're on the beach, lying on the sand, right on the ground. Let the full weight of your body fall onto the sand. You can feel it on your back and on your legs—soft, fine, and warm.

2

Now you begin to feel how the waves wash over the soles of your feet. You feel how the waves come and go, bathing your feet in salt water.

3

Then you begin to feel a warmth on your chest and on your cheeks—the rays of sunlight are warming you up and filling you with energy!

4

All of a sudden, a gentle breeze of fresh air caresses your face and whispers softly into your ear: *whooooooosshhhh*.

Now you feel relaxed and full of energy!

To the four elements—earth, water, fire, and air—thank you!

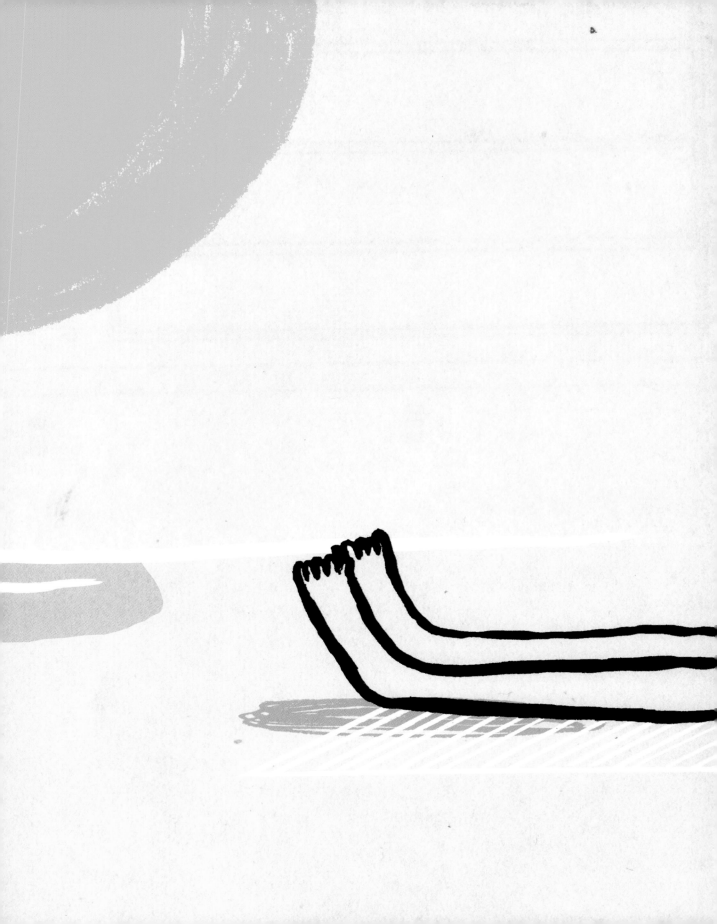

COLORED CLOUDS

1

Visualize the sky. See how the clouds go by?

Choose a white cloud, and start painting
it red—the color of anger. Think about all the
things that have made you angry today,
this week…

2

Paint the entire cloud red, do it angrily,
and then let it go. It moves away until it
disappears. This way, you let go of all
that annoyance.

Do the same thing for the color blue, the color
of sadness. Then do the same thing for black,
the color of fear. Then let those clouds go,
until sadness and fear disappear as well.

3

Imagine a green cloud, the color of calm.
A green mist begins to gently cover your feet,
slowly rising up your legs, your thighs…
until reaching your neck. Now your entire
body is colored green and is at peace.

4

A yellow ray of sunlight, the color
of happiness, lights up your face and makes
you smile.

You feel happy and at peace!

THE STARS

1

Lie down on the floor or on the bed, facing up, with your arms and legs spread out from your body, as if your body were a five-pointed star.

2

Now visualize a spot of white light at the center of your belly, above your belly button. Little by little, this light gradually becomes more intense and begins to spread all over your body: your belly, your chest, your arms, your legs, your head…until all five points of your body are completely illuminated.

You have become a star radiating white light!

3

See your radiance—brilliant, dazzling.
You begin to see other spots of light near you.
You realize that you're surrounded by stars,
which are all equally dazzling.

4

Look at yourself, shining in the dark sky.
You and the other stars are all part of the
vastness of the universe.

SUGGESTIONS FOR PRACTICE

Where:
The best place is somewhere with subdued lighting
and without any noise. But you can also practice in the classroom,
in the car, or outdoors. Anywhere you want! The important thing
is to practice.

When:
When your child needs to, whether because they're restless,
or anxious, or simply because they want to.

The best time to relax is at night, before going to bed. You can also
practice these exercises in the morning, to gather energy and focus.

How:
Visualizing is easier with the eyes closed. But if the child doesn't
want to close their eyes, it's no big deal. Don't force the issue;
visualizing with eyes open is fine, too.

Recommended Poses:
- *Sukhasana:* sitting cross-legged with the back straight.
This is an easy yoga pose for meditation.

- *Savasana:* lying down on the floor facing up, with the legs and
arms parallel to the body, and the palms of the hands facing up.
This is the yoga pose for total relaxation: it soothes and unites mind
and body. This pose is often the first step in the practice of meditation.

- Sitting down on a chair with the feet on the ground
and the hands resting on the legs.

SPAGHETTI

It is best for the child to be in the *savasana* pose, letting the full weight of their body fall onto the ground.

At the end of the visualization exercise, check that the child's arms and legs are relaxed and that they can be moved gently without offering any resistance.

A SPECIAL TREE

This can be done while seated, in the *sukhasana* pose, or in the *savasana* pose.

Afterwards, take a moment to talk about the visualization exercise, as long as your child is willing to do so. It is important for them to be able to share what they were thinking about, without any judgment. What did they hang up on the tree? What were their worries? What wish did they ask for? However, it is not advisable to pressure your child if they don't want to talk about it. The important thing is that they have gotten it out of their system.

THE BUTTERFLY

This can be done seated or lying down, but this is a good visualization exercise to do right before bedtime, while lying down on the bed.

THE FOUR ELEMENTS

This can be done while seated or lying down.

It is an exercise that helps to connect with nature and gives energy as well as peace. It is best when done in the morning or during the day.

COLORED CLOUDS

This can be done while seated or lying down.
This visualization exercise requires a little more time to do.
The child needs to visualize, think about what they want to let go of,
and "paint" the clouds. It is worthwhile to take a moment to ask
your child, "What makes you angry, sad, afraid…?"

Just like in the "Special Tree" visualization exercise, ask your child to
describe and share their experience with you, if they wish to do so.

THE STARS

This has to be done using the *savasana* pose, with the arms and legs
slightly separated from the body, forming a star.

It might be helpful for the child to place a small white light
on their belly. This way, they can imagine how that white light spreads
out over their entire body.

This is a meditation technique that goes from the tiniest detail
to the vastness of the universe. It connects the child with their inner
selves and the universe.

Mamen Duch, the founder of Yogui Kids (www.yoguikids.com), has been a yoga teacher for children since 2008—certified by Shari Vilchez-Blatt of Karma Kids Yoga in New York. She is also a yoga teacher for children with special needs, certified by Craig Hanauer after completing the Every Kid's Yoga training program. She received her degree in performing arts from the Institut del Teatre in 1991 and founded the company T de Teatre. She has worked as a film, theater, and television actress. She also trains teachers, educators, and actors. In addition, she works on social action projects related to yoga and theater. She is the author of the book *Maya y el yoga*.

Raúl Nieto Guridi was born in Seville and studied painting at the Faculty of Fine Arts there. Since then, he has worked in practically all fields of graphics, printing, design, and advertising. From 1995 onwards, he has specialized in graphic arts and the multimedia industry. Since 2010, his work has mainly focused on illustrations in children's publishing and posters for cultural campaigns involving theatre, dance, and puppets, as well as book covers for La Joie de Lire. He gives workshops on illustration and creativity. He also collaborates with several NGOs. His books have been translated into more than nine languages, and he has received several international illustration awards.